# HELP IS ON THE WAY FOR:

# Charts & Graphs

Written by Marilyn Berry
Pictures by Bartholomew

CHILDRENS PRESS ™

CHICAGO

Childrens Press
School and Library Edition

Executive Producer: Marilyn Berry
Editor: Theresa Tinkle
Consultants: Patricia Harrington and Terie Snyder
Design: Abigail Johnston
Typesetting: Curt Chelin

ISBN 0-516-03241-0
Copyright © 1985 by Marilyn Berry
Living Skills Productions, Fallbrook, CA
All rights reserved.
Printed in the United States of America

So you need to learn about **charts and graphs?**

Hang on! Help is on the way.

If you are having a hard time

- reading charts and graphs,
- knowing which types of charts and graphs to use, or
- making charts and graphs...

...you are not alone!

Just in case you're wondering...

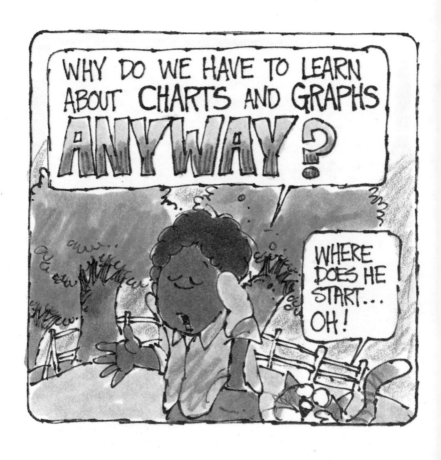

...why don't we start at the beginning?

# What Are Charts and Graphs?

Charts and graphs are drawings or diagrams that present information in a quick, easy-to-read form. Charts and graphs allow you to record a lot of information in a small amount of space.

# Why Are Charts and Graphs Important?

We get information from many different sources
such as:
- books
- newspapers
- magazines
- television

These sources often use charts and graphs to present
some of their information. To understand all the
information each source offers, you need to be able
to read the charts and graphs.

It is also important for you to know how to make your own charts and graphs.

You will find that charts and graphs can be helpful tools for

- Your personal use

- Your schoolwork

Charts and graphs are like puzzles. You need to figure out what pieces of information are involved and how they fit together.

There are simple formulas you can follow for both reading and making charts and graphs. It can be fun if you just take it one step at a time.

9

# Charts

There are two different types of charts. Each type serves a different purpose.

## Tables and Schedules

Tables and schedules list information that can be used over and over as a reference such as:
- a table of multiplication facts, or
- a bus schedule.

The information is listed in columns (that you read from top to bottom) and rows (that you read from left to right).

The parts of a table or schedule are:

| AGE GROUP | TIME | FIELD | COACH | TEAM NAME |
|-----------|------|-------|-------|-----------|
| 6-8 YRS | 9:00-11:00 | 1* | JONES | BLUE JAYS |
| 9-10 YRS | 9:00-11:00 | 2** | SMITH | HAWKS |
| 11-12 YRS | 11:00-12:00 | 1* | SIMMS | TIGERS |
| 13-14 YRS | 11:00-12:00 | 2** | FRANKS | BRAVES |

COLUMN TITLES
MAIN TITLE
Schedule for Baseball Tryouts
ROW TITLES
FACTS

\* FIELD 1 - HILLCREST PARK
\*\* FIELD 2 - GENERAL PARK

KEY TO SYMBOLS

Practice using this chart by finding the name of the field where a 12-year-old would go for baseball tryouts.

- Slide your finger down the row titles until you come to the row entitled ''11-12 yrs.''
- Slide your finger across that row until you reach the column entitled ''Field.''
- Your finger will be pointing to ''1*.''
- Look up the symbol (*) in the ''Key to Symbols'' and you will find the name of the field. The answer is Field 1 at Hillcrest Park.

11

# Progress Charts

Progress charts are used to record information as it is gathered. Some examples are:
- a schoolwork progress chart,
- a weather chart, and
- an expenses chart.

This type of chart is drawn with only the main title, the row titles, and the column titles filled in at the beginning. The rest of the information is filled in as it happens.

The parts of a progress chart are:

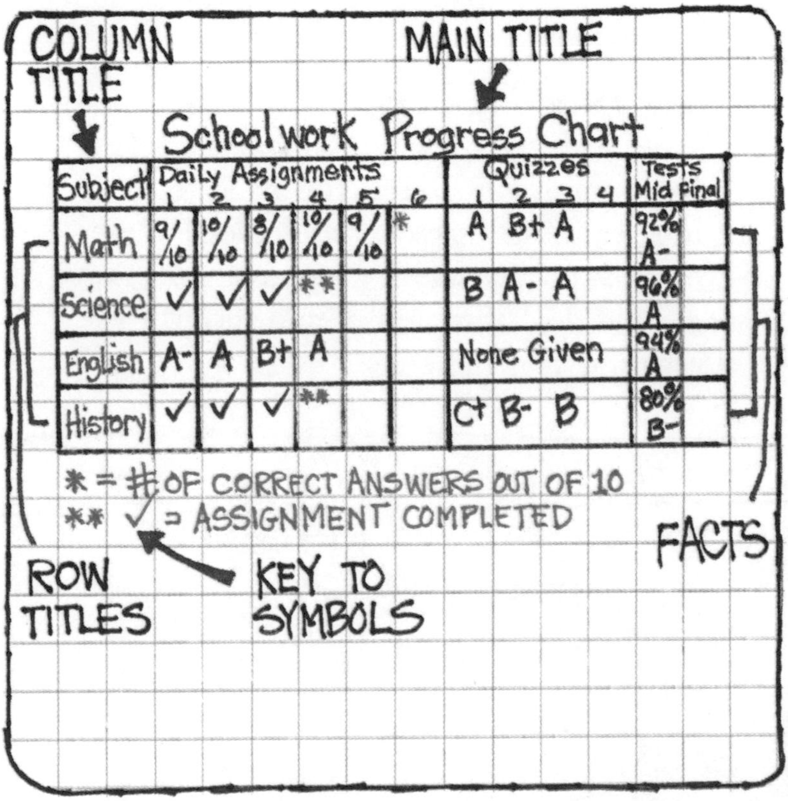

The chart shows:

| COLUMN TITLE (↓) | | | | | | | MAIN TITLE (↓) | | | |
|---|---|---|---|---|---|---|---|---|---|---|

**School work Progress Chart**

| Subject | Daily Assignments | | | | | | Quizzes | | | | Tests |
| | 1 | 2 | 3 | 4 | 5 | 6 | 1 | 2 | 3 | 4 | Mid Final |
|---|---|---|---|---|---|---|---|---|---|---|---|
| Math | 9/10 | 10/10 | 8/10 | 10/10 | 9/10 | * | A | B+ | A | | 92% A- |
| Science | ✓ | ✓ | ✓ | ** | | | B | A- | A | | 96% A |
| English | A- | A | B+ | A | | | None Given | | | | 94% A |
| History | ✓ | ✓ | ✓ | ** | | | C+ | B- | B | | 80% B- |

\* = # OF CORRECT ANSWERS OUT OF 10
\*\* ✓ = ASSIGNMENT COMPLETED

ROW TITLES → KEY TO SYMBOLS

FACTS

Practice using the chart by finding the grade that was given for the English test.

- Slide your finger down the row titles until you come to the row entitled "English."
- Slide your finger across that row until you reach the column entitled "Tests."
- Your finger will be pointing to "94% A," which is the answer.

## Making Your Own Chart

You can make your own chart by following four simple steps.

**Step One: Decide which type of chart you need.**
- You will want to make a **table or schedule** if you have information that you need to organize, and will use over and over.
- You will want to make a **progress chart** if you need to gather information, and record the information as it happens.

**Step Two: Decide on the basic parts of your chart.**
- Begin with the title. Ask yourself, "What do I hope to learn from this chart?"
- Decide on the main ingredients. You will need to decide on the column titles and the row titles. You can usually find these ingredients suggested in the main title. For example: Title—"After-School Time Chart." Ingredients—School *days* and after school *hours*.

**Step Three: Draw your chart.**
You will need
- graph paper,
- a ruler, and
- a pencil.

*Instructions:*
- Count the number of column titles you need and draw that many columns on your paper.
- Count the number of row titles you need and draw that many rows on your paper.
- Fill in the proper column and row titles.
- Write the title of your chart at the top of the page.

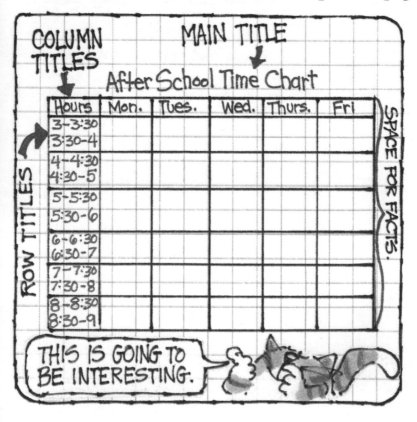

## Step Four: Fill in the facts on your chart.

*If you are making a table or schedule,* you can fill in the facts on your chart immediately. For example, for an "After-School Time Chart" you would

- make a plan for the best use of your time (include activities that are already planned such as dinner and chores),
- record your plan by filling in the facts on the chart, then
- use the chart as a guide for spending your time.

COLUMN TITLES

MAIN TITLE

After School Time Chart

| HOURS | Mon. | Tues. | Wed. | Thurs. | Fri. |
|---|---|---|---|---|---|
| 3-3:30 | Relax | Relax | Relax | Relax | Relax |
| 3:30-4 | Piano | Practice | Practice | Practice | Practice |
| 4-4:30 | //// | //// | //// | //// | //// |
| 4:30-5 | //// | //// | //// | //// | //// |
| 5-5:30 | //// | soccer | //// | soccer | //// |
| 5:30-6 | Drama | //// | Drama | //// | Drama |
| 6-6:30 | Dinner | Dinner | Dinner | Dinner | Dinner |
| 6:30-7 | Dishes | Dishes | Dishes | Dishes | Dishes |
| 7-7:30 | //// | //// | //// | //// | //// |
| 7:30-8 | //// | //// | //// | //// | //// |
| 8-8:30 | Freetime | Freetime | Freetime | Freetime | Freetime |
| 8:30-9 | Bedtime | Bedtime | Bedtime | Bedtime | Bedtime |

ROW TITLES

FACTS

KEY: ////  AVAILABLE STUDY TIME

KEY TO SYMBOLS

17

If you are making a progress chart, you will not fill the chart in all at once. Instead, you will fill in the facts as they happen. To be completely accurate, you may want to keep your chart with you and record your activities at the end of each hour. Once your chart is completed, you will have gathered a lot of interesting information.

Many times there will be more information in a chart than you see at first glance. For example, an "After-School Time Chart" can tell you

- how much total time is spent on each activity, and .
- how the time spent on one activity compares with the time spent on a different activity.

Another way to find this out is to put the information on a graph.

# Graphs

There are four different types of graphs:
- the line graph,
- the bar graph,
- the circle graph, and
- the pictograph.

Each type of graph serves a different purpose and displays information in a different way. Here are examples of each type of graph:

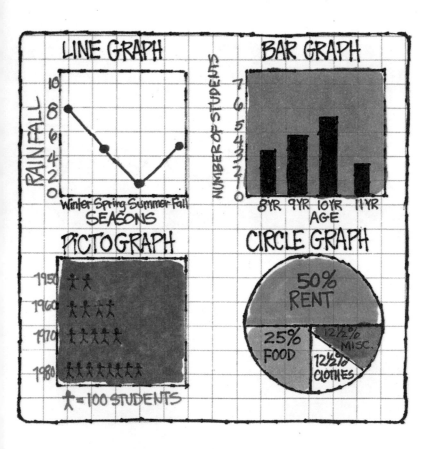

# How to Read Graphs

There are three different types of information you will need to look for when reading a graph.

1. **The general information** gives you an overview of what you can expect to find in the graph.
2. **The specific information** includes the actual information that is plainly stated in the graph.
3. **The suggested information** is information not actually stated in the graph but is "suggested" by the other information.

## Reading a Line Graph

The line graph is one of the easiest graphs to read. It is especially useful for showing change over a period of time.

**1. The general information.** For an overview of the line graph, you need to study its basic parts.

- Read the main title. This tells you what the graph is about.
- Read the titles on the vertical axis (the line running from top to bottom).
- Read the titles on the horizontal axis (the line running from left to right).
- Read the source of information. This tells you how reliable the information is.
- Read the key to the symbols. This tells you how the symbols are used in the graph.

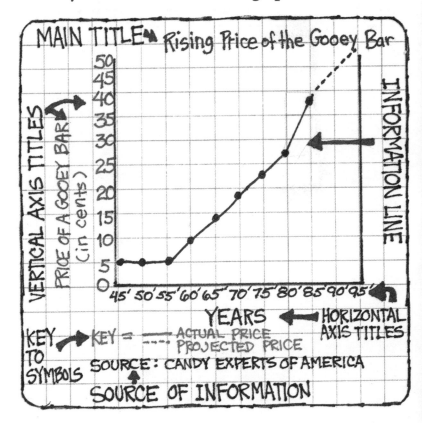

**2. The specific information** is found on the
information line. Practice using the information
line by finding the price of a Gooey Bar in 1965.

- Slide your finger along the horizontal axis until
  you come to the title "1965."
- Slide your finger straight up until you reach the
  information line.
- Slide your finger to the left until you reach the
  vertical axis.
- Your finger will be pointing to the answer,
  which is 15 cents.

**3. The suggested information.** You can practice looking for suggested information by studying the graph on page 23 and asking questions such as:

- How has the price of a Gooey Bar changed since 1950? *Answer:* The price has increased.
- If the change that is shown on the chart continues, what will happen? *Answer:* The price will continue to increase.

### Reading a Bar Graph
The bar graph is also a simple graph to read. This type of graph is especially useful for comparing information.

**1. The general information.** For an overview of the bar graph, you need to study its basic parts.

- Read the main title. What is the graph about?
- Read the vertical and horizontal axis titles. What kinds of information are presented?
- Read the source of information. Is it reliable?
- Read the key to the symbols. How are the symbols used?

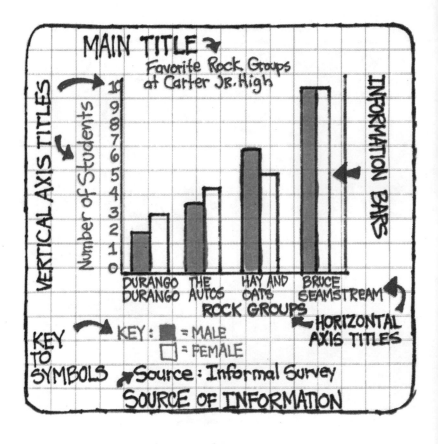

**2. The specific information** is found in the information bars. Practice using the information bars by finding the number of males who chose "The Autos" as the best rock group.

- Slide your finger along the horizontal axis until you come to the title "The Autos."
- Using the key, find the bar that represents males.
- Slide your finger up to the top of the bar.
- Slide your finger to the left until you reach the vertical axis.
- Your finger will be pointing to the answer, which is 4 males.

**3. The suggested information.** You can practice looking for suggested information by studying the graph on page 27 and asking questions such as:

- Who would probably sell the most records at Carter Jr. High? *Answer:* Bruce Seamstream.
- Is there a big difference in musical taste between the girls and the boys? *Answer:* No. The tastes seem to be very similar.

## Reading a Pictograph

The pictograph can be a fun type of graph to read. Instead of using bars to represent the information, the pictograph uses pictures or symbols. It is also used to compare information.

**1. The general information.** For an overview of
the pictograph, you need to study its basic parts.
- Read the main title. What is the graph about?
- Read the vertical axis titles. What kind of
  information is presented?
- Read the key to the symbols. How are the
  symbols used?
- Read the source of the information. Is it
  reliable?

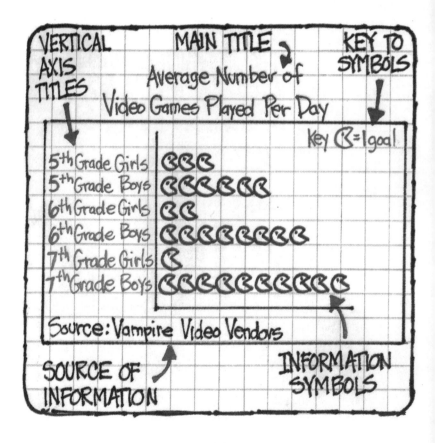

**2. The specific information** is found in the information symbols. Practice using the information symbols by finding the average number of video games 7th grade boys play per day.

- Slide your finger down the vertical axis until you come to the title "7th Grade Boys."
- Slide your finger to the right and count the symbols in the row.
- Multiply the number of symbols (10) by the value of the symbol in the key (1): 10 × 1 = 10. *Answer:* The 7th grade boys play an average of 10 games a day.

**3. The suggested information.** You can practice looking for suggested information by studying the graph on page 31 and asking questions such as:

- Who plays more video games—girls or boys? *Answer:* According to this graph—boys.
- What changes take place as the girls and boys get older? *Answer:* The girls play less, and the boys play more.

## Reading a Circle Graph

The circle graph is sometimes called a pie graph. This type of graph is especially useful when you need to show how a whole is divided into parts. Circle graphs are usually based on percentages.

- The whole circle = 100%
- Each segment is assigned a percentile value. The size of the segment is drawn to match that percentile.
- All the segments must add up to 100%

**1. The general information.** For an overview of the circle graph, you need to study its basic parts.

- Read the main title. What is the graph about?
- Read the segment titles. What does each part of the circle stand for?

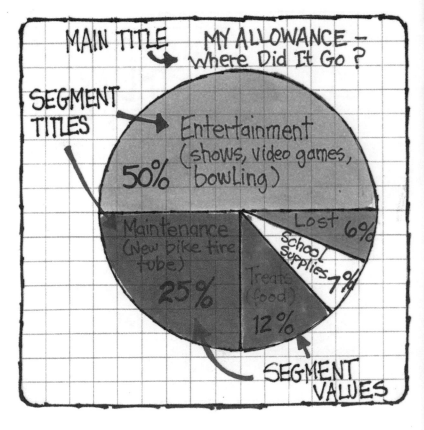

MAIN TITLE  MY ALLOWANCE — where Did It Go?

SEGMENT TITLES

Entertainment (shows, video games, bowling) 50%

Maintenance (New bike tire tube) 25%

Lost 6%

School Supplies 7%

Treats (food) 12%

SEGMENT VALUES

**2. The specific information.** Locating the specific information on a circle graph is easy. Simply read each segment title and identify the value assigned to each segment. You can practice by finding out how much of the allowance was spent on entertainment.

- Locate the segment entitled ''Entertainment.''
- Look at the percentile assigned to that segment. *Answer:* 50% of the allowance was spent on entertainment.

**3. The suggested information.** You can practice looking for suggested information by studying the graph on page 35 and asking questions such as:

- What was most of the allowance spent on?
  *Answer:* Entertainment.
- How much money was put into savings?
  *Answer:* None.

# Making Your Own Graphs

To make most graphs you will need
- graph paper,
- a ruler, and
- a pencil.

You can make your own graph by following these simple steps.

**Step One: Decide which type of graph you need.**
- If you want to show change over a period of time, make a line graph.
- If you want to compare information, make a bar graph or a pictograph.
- If you need to show how a "whole" is divided into "segments," make a circle graph.

**Step Two: Decide on the basic parts of your graph.**

- Begin with the title. "Ask yourself, "What major question will my graph answer?"
- Next, gather the information. Ask yourself, "What information do I need in order to complete my graph?"
- Divide the information into two categories, or sets. This will help you plot the information on your graph.

# Step Three: Draw your graph.

*Instructions for making a line graph:*
- Study one set of information. Figure out the title for your horizontal axis ("game number") and plot the game numbers on your graph.
- Study the other set of information. Figure out the title for your vertical axis ("number of goals scored") and plot the numbers on your graph.
- Record the information at the proper points on your graph and connect the points with a line. For example, above the first game, put a point at the "2." This shows they scored two goals during the first game.